# KINGDOM KIDS

# RAMEL MOORE

KINGDOM KIDS

Ramel Moore
Pastormel@fortifiedlife.church

ISBN 978-1-949826-42-5

Printed in the USA.
All rights reserved

Published by: EAGLES GLOBAL BOOKS | Frisco, Texas
In conjunction with the 2022 Eagles Authors Course
**Cover & interior designed by DestinedToPublish.com**

# DEDICATION

Shirley x Moore, my first book is dedicated to you. Not only did you sign me up for this course without even asking me, but you also supported me through every step of this process, from reading my manuscript to helping me think things through to being tech support and helping me with Microsoft Word, Acrobat and any other program I used to write this book. You are the best partner, teammate and wife a man can ask for. There probably wouldn't be a book without you, definitely not at this time. So, I just want to say I appreciate you, I honor you and I thank you for who you are and your constant contribution to my life. Love you, Lifey.

# TABLE OF CONTENTS

# INTRODUCTION

*"I tell you the truth, anyone who believes in me will do the same works I have done, and even greater works, because I am going to be with the Father."*

What is it? Is it that we don't believe, or are we just too afraid? These are just a couple of the questions I think about and two of the many thoughts that have sparked the heart for this book. Why are God's people not the innovators, the architects, the creators, the thought-provoking builders, the inventors, the influencers, the leaders and masterminds? I know one thing: it's *not* because that's not what God wants for us or how he intended it to be.

As I study the Word of God, I can't help but think about all the promises God presents to us through his Word. Then all the questions start to plague my mind about why and who and how we can began to live in the fullness of God's glory, and how we can reign here on earth. You see, I'm wired to be a natural-born competitor as a former Division III college basketball player and now a basketball coach for the last 15 years. I'm naturally competitive. I want to win, and I want to be the best. Naturally, I also want anyone I come in contact with to win and be the best, to succeed and meet their full potential.

So, when I read the Bible, I can't help but be challenged. I can't help but see what can potentially be, and begin to desire the "more" that God has for us. You see, the great part about the Bible is that we know the outcome of the story. If you don't know, the answer is that we win! I completely understand that the victory is ours through Jesus. But are we called to do more and be more while we are here on earth? Is my calling and purpose being fulfilled if I'm just okay with what awaits me on the other side, or is there more to be had, accomplished and orchestrated by the kids of the kingdom? What does it look like if we are the heads and not the tails? If we are the lenders and not the borrowers? If men and women of God are the CEOs, the source of innovation, leading influencers? I know we are just visitors, I know this is not our home, but I also know the power that lives inside of us.

I'm just a high school basketball coach, a pastor of a small church, a business owner, a husband and father, a simple man with some big ideas, some plaguing questions and a fire inside of me that just can't let go of some of these scriptures I read without attempting to at least explore their possibilities. Let's be clear, I'm well aware of the great exploits of the ones that have come before me. But what kind of coach, pastor, forward thinker would I be if I didn't think we can do more, build more, heal more, create more, lift the name of Jesus higher and represent the kingdom greater? One of my mentors, Apostle Fashaw, always says miracles are easy for God, and I believe that to be a fact. My hope is that this book not only sparks your desire to maximize your full self in God but also shows you biblical strategies and guides that can lead you to the greatest version of you.

This book is strategically designed to guide God's people to living a maximized kingdom life, helping them get from where they are to where God wants them to be by focusing our attention on offense instead of defense. It will help you, the reader, identify your identity in Christ, your purpose on earth and the opportunities that present themselves when you tap into your God-given calling. My hope for this book is to encourage, empower and embolden you to maximize Holy Spirit in your everyday life and take your rightful position as God intended. This book will guide God's people on how to get unstuck and also catapult into destiny, all while creating legacy. We will be guided on this journey by scriptures and true testimonies, all wrapped in Coach Mel style, offering you a practical, easy-to-digest, Spirit-filled conversation.

As we go on this journey together, we will map out and discover the treasures that God himself has placed in his children. I can't lie to you, this journey will not be for everyone. But if you are a person who believes in thriving and not just striving, who believes that a part of being obedient to God is being a fruit-bearing tree, is being a instrument in the Father's hand that is yielding to the beautiful notes of the master musician, or being the clay that is okay with being stretched, bent, molded and filled with the gift that never runs out, then this book is for you. This book is for the multipliers, for the secret creators. Let this book coach you to walk in the promises that God has perfectly sprinkled throughout the Word. If you want more, let's go there together. Tap in, open up, release, explore with me. Let's go!

# FOUNDATION

"A strong foundation is a wise man's
first victory."

Have you ever wondered to yourself, "Am I living the life God intended me to live? Am I going the way he wants me to go? Am I doing what he wants me to do, or am I just living and doing what I think I should be doing or what society says I should be doing? Am I just following trends, or is this life I'm living just me rehearsing something that I stole from somewhere else? Is this who I am, or am I just wearing a different costume every day? Is this a mask of who I believe I'm supposed to be?"

Questions like these are raised when inquisitive curiosity meets unsatisfied urges and a conflicted soul. You ask these questions because you don't know who you are, and what you are piecing together is based on borrowed beliefs. At some point, we have all had a void in our being that needs to be filled by purpose and identity. Before we ever find where we are going and what we should be doing in life, we first have to understand that who we are, our true identity, will always be our compass. If you are not sure of who you are, you will never be sure of where you are going, and you will never fully understand who you are until you learn *whose* you are!

I know this is the beginning of the book, and I hate to get so deep so quick, but I don't believe in building without a proper foundation. Matthew 7:24-27 talks about building on a solid foundation, so let's get deep, let's dig a little, let's set our foundation! Who are you? Whose are you? And who does God say you are? Answering these questions will serve as your foundation, because your identity in Christ also serves as your "why." Answering these questions helps you to navigate through life. It's kind of like a compass: whenever you feel lost, you just use your identity compass to track back to who you are.

Also, when you answer the questions "Who am I?" and "Whose am I?" you don't leave room for misinterpretations or any other foreign influences that may try to come to define you. When we're clear on who we are, we leave no space for imposter syndrome. Establishing identity fortifies you. This knowledge creates a strong fortress between you and the doubt and unbelief that wants to take residence in your mind simply to produce confusion and unclarity, which are doors for the enemy to taint how you view yourself.

So, let's answer some of these questions. Who are you? You are a child of God. Galatians 3:26 (NLT) tells us: "*For you are all children of God through faith in Christ Jesus.*" This is the foundation that you must build your house upon. If you can find yourself here every time, it will be very difficult to ever get lost. When you identify as a child of God, you are then saying that you are like your Maker – you share in his character. If you are not sure if you are a child of God, ask yourself this simple question: Have you given your heart to God? Have you confessed with your mouth and believe in your heart that Jesus is Lord? If the answer is no, there's no better time than now to repeat this prayer:

"Heavenly Father, I come to you in prayer asking you to forgive me of my sins. I believe that your Son Jesus is Lord and he died on the cross for me that I might be forgiven and have eternal life in the kingdom of heaven. I believe that he rose from the dead on the third day for me. I ask you right now to come into my life and be my personal Lord and Savior. I am cleansed in his blood and I am saved. In Jesus' name, Amen!"

If you said that prayer, first of all, welcome to the family! Secondly, now you can truly call yourself a child of God, and now your new life begins. Remember, when you are a child of God, you now identify as such in word and in action. This is not perfection; this is just the foundation, the launching pad to the rest of your new life. This new relationship is the greatest relationship you will ever have. Just being in communion with God creates traits and characteristics in us that will keep us. You now have a new author to your documentary. Your story will now be different.

Think about it like this. Whoever raised you or whoever you grew up around will influence you. I don't care how hard you try not to be like them when you get older, you just can't help it. You constantly see similarities – it's just the way it is. You may walk like them or talk like them; your subtle mannerisms are inevitable. You spent so much time around them that you can't escape it. It's the same with your Heavenly Father. Imagine if you spent time with the one who created the universe. I mean, you spent your life with Al Senior and you learned how to belch Christmas songs and tie nine different types of knots. But now you are a child of the King of all Kings, the God of the universe – that relationship should impact your life at a far greater level.

If you are not sold yet, let's go back to the beginning. If you want to know where your identity came from, you must start with God the Father. The Bible says in Genesis 1:27 that we were made in the image of God, so not only are we children of God, but we were made in his image and his likeness. This means we were made to be like God. When you gave your life to God, that was just you outwardly being reconciled to your Heavenly Father.

Now, I know for a lot of people, it may make you feel a little uncomfortable to think that God made us, and made us like himself. But think about why that makes you uncomfortable. Could it be the pressure that hearing this puts on you, or could it be that you have a hard time seeing yourself in such a way? I completely understand that the bodies that we live in make it very difficult to comprehend that we have God's natural characteristics and abilities. Like our Maker, we were made to create, invent, build, populate. We were born with dominion and power. We are royal heirs to the throne.

I know it's much easier to embrace having the character of our earthly father or mother. We can see their strengths and their flaws. Some of us have spent significant time with our parents and can clearly see the resemblance. And that's my point exactly: we are called to build relationship with our Heavenly Father as well as spend time with him so that we can eventually see ourselves in him and he can see himself in us. The goal is to be so much like Christ that we are seen like him here on earth. Through prayer, the Word and worship, we will begin to see the resemblance. As we get closer to God, we will also become increasingly more anointed, influential and potent. Our goal should be to become more like our Father, to be light and salt shining in dark places and bringing flavor to places that lack God's influence. The more we become like him, the more we will become at peace with who we are and what we are called to do on this earth.

I don't care who you are. If you hang with anyone long enough and you study them, you will naturally take on some traits and mannerisms.

One of our main jobs on the earth is to learn our identity. And the way we learn identity is by learning who God is. When we learn who he is, we also learn who we are. This is step one in building a firm foundation. This is where we begin to build a life with purpose, direction and meaning. This is where we begin to cultivate legacy. This is where we begin to make a great impact here on earth. Maximizing your time here on earth comes through your identity, and your identity comes through your relationship with God!

What does this all mean? When you are secure in yourself and are clear on your identity and who you are, you never suffer from identity crisis. You don't waste time trying to be like other people, and you never believe what others say about you. If it doesn't align with what God has said about you, then it can't be true. You are always betting on you because of who you belong to. Because you clearly understand the power and privilege that comes with being a kid of the King, you move different. You move with reverence and direction, you move with grace and dignity. You understand your responsibility as an influencer, innovator and creative. But more importantly, you live with direction, constantly standing on your post, knowing that you were born to do greater works, fully committed to God's will being fulfilled in your life.

It's never performance; it's always preference. You always choose God. You always choose to walk in your calling. When you are on your post and you are maximizing your calling, you are actually worshiping

God with your life, and that's what we are called to do. Let's live in the freedom that our identity in Christ gives us, because who the Son sets free is free indeed. Let's never return to the bondage of not knowing who we are, the bondage of doubt and confusion. Let's live a life full of fruit, full of purpose and praise through a lifestyle that reflects the will of God in our life. But let's live in the Grace that was given to us, knowing that our foundation is secure and now we can begin to build on the rock called Jesus.

Here are five things people with strong foundations say:

1. Lord, not my will but your will be done in my life.
2. Lord, have your way in my life.
3. Lord, I yield to your Spirit.
4. Lord, you are first. I prioritize your ways.
5. Bless my coming in and my going out.

Here are five things people with strong foundations have:

1. Integrity
2. Fortitude
3. Solid principles
4. Flexibility
5. Support systems

C H A P T E R 2

# WHO'S YOUR DADDY?

*"You will always begin to reflect
the things you spend the most time
with, so spend your time wisely."*

What makes me a kingdom kid? This is a great question, and I'm so glad you asked. The simple answer is that your relationship with the King is what determines if you're a kingdom kid. It's your ability to first recognize that you were made and created for relationship with God the Father, and it just so happens that God the Father is also the King. This is what makes you a kingdom kid. What you do with that info is up to you, and we will get deeper into leveraging that relationship later on in this book.

Think about it like this: We've all seen those movies of old that are set in a kingdom, and there's a bunch of kids playing outside who are seemingly just playing, but really they are acting. They are playing the roles that they have seen around the kingdom. Normally, those kids are the children of people in authority in the kingdom, usually connected to the king in some way. The deeper their understanding of their parents' role in the kingdom, the greater their character can be. It's just like us – the greater our relationship is with the King, the more we have insight and revelation, and therefore a firm footing into what our character should look like. This then allows us to strive for greater relationship, which in return makes for greater character. Your character shapes your identity, and that's what makes us a kingdom kid or not.

The deeper answer to this question is our ability not only to recognize our connection to the kingdom of God through direct relationship with the King but also to fully understand the dominion and power we possess because of that relationship. All dominion, power and authority belongs to the King – that's what makes him the King, and that's what makes it a kingdom. Think about it like this: If your dad was a police officer, you would be a cop's kid; if your dad was a preacher, you would be a preacher's kid. No difference here – your dad is the King, which means he has a kingdom. The fortunate part for you is that your dad is the King of all kings. So, because of your adoption, that gives you the title of kingdom kid and the rights to everything that comes with that.

To identify as a kingdom kid, yes, you must know who Abba is, and you must build a solid relationship and have continual communion with God, but in that process of getting closer to God, he will inevitably began to renew your mind. This renewal is called the kingdom mindset. For example, if you think about the awareness of who your King is as being like a car, then your kingdom mindset is the engine. You cannot be a kingdom kid without having a kingdom mindset. In order to share in the authority and dominion that comes with being an heir to the throne as a kingdom kid, you must surely share in the heart of the King.

The Bible tells us to renew our mind. It says that our thoughts are different from God's thoughts – actually, it says they are very different. This is the very reason why we are told to renew our mind – because we are to become more like Christ through our mindset, our heart posture. In order to be a kingdom kid, you must begin by accepting your identity in Christ and then begin to surrender a far inferior mindset for an open, endless, revelatory, connected kingdom mindset. This will be the thing that separates you the most from other people. This mindset is also what guides and influences your perspective and fuels your movements.

The Bible says that as a man thinks, so he is (Proverbs 23:7). So, that means kingdom kids think like kingdom kids. Well, what does it mean to think like a kingdom kid? To understand the mindset, we first have to understand the heart of the king. But before we go there, let's take a step back. What is kingdom? Kingdom is dominion, it's power, it's royalty and holiness, it's fortified. Knowing all that helps us to understand what a kingdom mindset is. It's a mind fueled by possibility, all based in faith and the power of Holy Spirit. It's regulated, backed and fortified by scripture. It's a mind that is forward thinking and not held back by wordly standards or regulations. It's a mind that understands royalty, dominion and power but is humble and understands godly order. A kingdom mindset allows the host to see life differently. A kingdom mindset always has foresight, insight and revelation because, again, it's shaped by the word of God and led by Holy Spirit. For example, people with a kingdom mindset have a clear understanding of the concept "It's better to give than to receive." Why? Because people with a kingdom mindset understand concepts like seed and harvest. People with a kingdom mindset think a balanced past, present and future are all important. Learning from your past and staying tapped into your current so you can be prepared for your future are all kingdom-minded concepts.

I could go on and on for days about what a kingdom mindset looks like, but one of the main things we must understand is that a kingdom mindset is a "service first" mindset. It's not self-seeking but truly fueled by love – or, in another translation, charity. It's fueled by giving and sacrifice. For most, this may be a culture clash or go against the grain. Most of what was taught to us is that in order to get, you need to go get it, whereas in the kingdom, it's the complete opposite: In order to get, you must sow, you must give. In the kingdom, the first shall be last and the last shall be first.

Understanding that, you will begin to wrap your life around what you can do for others versus what you can do for yourself. In order to be a true kingdom kid, this must be a part of your DNA. This is the heart of all we do, of all we are. We will live with the understanding that success is impossible without sacrifice and, more importantly, without charity. If I live my whole life getting for myself and I never bless others, I have nothing! But if I'm constantly sowing into others, then I must be constantly reaping a harvest. That's the only way I can continue to give. Think about it like this: Imagine if everyone didn't care about themselves, but they cared about the needs of others. You wouldn't be able to go anywhere and not be taken care of, and no one would ever be left out because we would only care about others. I know I'm a weirdo in this world where consideration, empathy and giving are so foreign. Thinking about a world where those things are first on people's minds is a little off, but why? Why is that off? It's because we need to renew our thinking to match the rules and customs of the kingdom.

"You cannot be a blessing without first being blessed."

Let's take a moment to reflect and answer these questions:

1. How is your relationship with God?
2. When you think of God, what comes to mind first – King, Lord, Father, or something else?
3. Does your life look like you are a son or daughter of the King from Monday through Saturday?

4. Do you spend valuable time with God?
5. Do you live with a defensive or offensive mindset?

So, now that we understand what a kingdom kid is, let's dive into what that means to the world.

# ME ON EARTH

"Understanding your purpose
is the shortcut to everywhere."

We are called by Christ to be ambassadors of the kingdom of God, which means we need to represent dominion and authority. We are called to be the head and not the tail, above and not beneath. We are called to be lenders and not borrowers, to be innovators, inventors, influencers. Kingdom kids understand their value. They find their value in what's in them as well as what's on them, meaning that when you are a child of God, you are filled with his Spirit. When you are filled with the Spirit of God, you are filled with the supernatural power of the Spirit. For most people, this concept is hard to believe about humans. How can your average person become a supernatural human? We see Marvel and DC comics and movies and get a distorted picture, or shall I say, those images are exaggerated. But our superpower through the Holy Spirit is found in the form of strategy, innovation, peace in pressure, strength in storms. It's found in the form of light and salt and the ability to see life clearly, to identify your purpose and others' and to live in it with grace and vigor. Your superpower allows you to lead at high levels to direct others to victory.

Kingdom kids are servants of the kingdom and of each other. Kingdom kids understand that one of our greatest superpowers is the ability to love – true love, without conditions. Have you ever watched gymnastics and said, "Wow, how can they do that?" It comes from countless hours in the gym perfecting their craft. It comes from blood, sweat and tears, from disappointment and struggle. This is what it takes to get what you see at the Olympics. Now think about that same thing, but your coach/trainer is God in the form of Holy Spirit, and your platform is not the Olympics but life. We are called to transform this world through being salt (meaning giving flavor( and light (meaning dispelling darkness). That's our super power, and we all have it, but we all need to develop it through blood, sweat and tears, through lots of failing and getting back up better than ever, through learning from each and every season, learning to love being in the gym of life.

Remember, we have a enemy whose purpose is to steal, kill and destroy. He is never after you, per se; he is always after your purpose. He knows that his time is running short, and that's all I will say about him in this book. Hold fast to the calling that God has placed on your life. Protect it by being active in it and continuously developing it through growing, which comes from learning, which comes from failing and perseverance.

# ALL THINGS BELONG TO GOD

"Before there was a Google,
there was a God."

You cannot truly be a kingdom kid if you are not constantly in the process of complete surrender. Kingdom kids give everything to God. Every endeavor, every career change, every idea is submitted to the board of the kingdom. Every business, every school decision, everything you do must belong to God. Not just a portion of it – the whole thing.

I learned this lesson the hard way. My first business I started about 15 years ago was just that: my first business. I started an AAU basketball organization. If you don't know what AAU is, it's the Amateur Athletic Union. Basically, it's travel basketball. You gather all the best middle school and high school players from your state and surrounding states, and you compete nationally in your age group. We were traveling all over the country and winning at a high level, and it was the largest program in Rhode Island, with three teams for every age group.

This thing was growing and flourishing, or so I thought. Just one problem: The organization, which started with just two teams, grew too fast. I thought I could solve my growth issue by getting more coaches. What started with just a passion to coach had now become so much more. The only problem is that not only did I never consult with God on this journey, I never added him to the fabric of what was being constructed. I learned really quickly that my ideas and ambitions, although they may be good, are nothing without God. I am 100% positive that my organization fell completely apart because it wasn't held together by what the owner stood for. I was separating the business from the God who gave me the business. How could I serve God every day except when it came to my business?

The truth of the matter is I was a hypocrite, only seeking God for what I thought he should be a part of, not grasping the fact that everything belongs to him. My business failing taught me everything I needed to know about being a kingdom kid: that if God is not in it, I'm not going to be either. If you're a lawyer, pray for your cases. If you're a doctor, pray for your patients. Ask God to take control of your practice, no matter what field you are in. Let God drive, lead and influence you – that's what being a kingdom kid truly is. I made the silly mistake of thinking that God could only be a part of godly things, without having a clear understanding that everything was made by and for him! Boy, was I mistaken. If you want what you touch to be a success, if you want to be significant in this world, if you are a true kingdom kid, your goal should always be focused on making God famous, making Jesus a commodity. The only way you can do that is if you put your hand on top of God's.

Not to mention I had no clue what godly things were. I was under the weird impression that if it wasn't in the church, then it wasn't his. The Bible says that God's kingdom should reign on earth as it is in heaven – it doesn't say "reign in church as it is in heaven." The way God reigns on earth is through our businesses, our practices, our complete lives, not just what we want to give him. We must allow God's power in us to reign through us in the world, in tech, sports, theater, medical fields, education, government. You name it, God should be there through his sons and daughters holding up the flag of the kingdom, representing God in all we do, being the salt and the light.

Don't be like me – don't limit God's access through ignorance if you want true success and significance in what you do. God wants to be present in you and in all you do. My first business blunder is one that, fortunately, I was able to learn from. Now I do everything with God. Every business I started after that one belongs to him. It belongs to the kingdom. If we were to be honest, we would have nothing without him, so it only makes sense to partner with him. *"In all your ways acknowledge Him, and He will direct your paths"* (Proverbs 3:6 NKJV). The key word in this verse is "all." That's what being a true kingdom kid is all about – acknowledging him in all we do, and allowing him to lead and be the best business partner we could ever ask for. Besides, we should feel honored that he allows us to be a part of the process to build whatever we are attempting to build, because he doesn't need us, we need him.

# MAXIMIZING ME

"The only way to do it correctly
is do it to the max."

I was 15 years old, and I had just moved from New York. I was looking for a place to play basketball, so I went to the first park I could find, which just happened to be near my house at the time. After playing at that park for a while, I realized I wasn't seeing new faces and I wasn't really being challenged. I was easily the best player, and honestly, it wasn't a place where real ball players went. It was close to home, it was familiar and I was great there, but I wanted more. So, I asked around to see where the competition was, and quickly they showed me the way. Maybe they were tired of me being the best at that court, or maybe they knew I should be playing against better players.

I went to this new court, and boy did I quickly realize I was at the wrong place in the beginning, and how much playing on those bent 8-foot rims with those guys in jean shorts and boots made my game worse. It took less skill to be the best there; it was no challenge. Now that I was at this new spot where I had to actually break a sweat, I understood quickly that being the best looks different depending who you are around. To truly be great, you have to get in the right atmosphere to maximize your abilities, and you cannot do that by being comfortable and playing small – it only comes through being challenged, stretched and surrounded by people who are better than you. This was the beginning of learning who I was called to be and really getting a hunger for learning my identity and being passionate about pursuing a purposeful, complete and maximized life.

One of the first keys to a maximized life is understanding who you are and where you are in life. I can't stress enough how important purpose and identity are. How can you maximize or grow in something if you don't know what you should be growing in? When I moved from New York, to Rhode Island I knew I wanted to be the best basketball player around, and although that was a temporary goal, it guided me to better myself in that area. That was my purpose, my "why," and that's what I pursued. Your goal should always be how to become the best version of yourself, how to become the expert of your life.

Let's be clear, you have already experienced some monumental moments up to this point, so your expertise is already solidified. But now it's time to maximize the values that have come from your experiences. Being a kingdom kid does not end at discovery – that's only the beginning. Life does not start until one discovers its purpose, and once that sometimes lifelong, vigorous and painful pursuit is final, then that's when the real fun begins of learning how to maximize the gift of you! Once you understand who you are, it makes it a whole lot easier to begin the journey of maximization. You won't need to keep going back and forth about whether you are worthy or what your purpose is. You are clear in who you are and why you are here. You are here to add kingdom to everything that your hands touch, and if it's kingdom, it's already special. Let me help you on this journey of maximization by giving you a few non-negotiables to getting everything that's in you out!

# 1. HOLY SPIRIT

The same Holy Spirit that helped you discover who you really are and what your purpose is here on earth will be the same power source that helps you stretch your natural abilities to a place that you can't even imagine. We have natural limits, so when we can't do something because of those limitations, Holy Spirit acts like a backup generator when the power goes out. It's also the clue when you are clueless, it's the map and the compass when you start to feel lost, it's the regulator of emotions.

Listen, in order for anyone to live to the max, they would need to yield to the "super" to go with the "power." Knowing your purpose comes with built-in power. To maximize that power, you must add the super to that – and that, my friend, can only come from Holy Spirit. It's the difference between a idea and a million-dollar company. It's the difference between a written song and a full album that is toured all over the world. We have the natural ability to create; Holy Spirit gives us the power to take that creativity to levels that are God-sized.

If maximization is your goal, you are off to a great start now that you have linked up with Holy Spirit. Now you must yield to the power that can get you to your goal. Kingdom is adding Holy Spirit, and Holy

Spirit is adding the super to the power. That's what makes everything superior and royal, that's what gives it dominion and validity, that's what makes it your best. In order to maximize, you must contain insight and foresight, which produces innovation. True innovation comes from seeing past what's in front of you, and that is generated by Holy Spirit.

In order to maximize, you must be able to sustain, maintain and gain fortification. Fortification is a gift that comes with Holy Spirit and is a key in maximization. How can you maximize if you are constantly spending time debugging, rebuilding and cleaning? Holy Spirit serves as a firewall there to protect and alert you to dangers that come to slow you down from meeting your full potential or break you down to stop you altogether. The amount of benefits Holy Spirit brings is virtually limitless – actually, it *is* limitless. Holy Spirit gives us a mindset that desires greater, that pushes for bigger. It is the imagination of our heart.

Let me give you just a few more examples. Imagine being a professional athlete but not having the trainers to help with recovery, the coaches to direct you, the lawyers to make sure you are not being taken advantage of, the accountants to keep it financially stable, the assistants to keep you on track, and I'm sure I'm missing a few folks. That's a big team to ensure you are able to get the most out of your gift. The only problem is, all those people are invested in your gift, and in order for them to continue, your gift must continue. Think of Holy Spirit as all those people wrapped up in one, but fully invested in you, not your gift, and also with the ability to enhance your gift and give you the power to clearly discern who else is supposed to be a part of this journey.

Remember, once I learned to add God to my business, the clarity of who I needed to have around me became evident. My ability to yield to the knowledge, wisdom and guidance of Holy Spirit gave me sorting power. It also gave me the drive I needed to get back, the drive to be great, the drive my dad used to create in me when I was a kid He would say, "Son, if you're going to do it, you might as well be the best." This is a great segue to my next non-negotiable to maximizing you.

## 2. YOUR TEAM

Have you ever heard the saying "You are only as strong as the team around you"? That statement is one of the truest statements ever, along with "It takes a village to raise a child." Well, if we are talking about being kingdom kids, then we must be talking about team, because all true kingdom kids understand the value of team and understand that there is no kingdom without the fluidity that comes from collaboration and unity. Kingdom kids understand that collaboration and teamwork are imperative to maximizing one's ability. Kingdom kids seek out opportunities to meet new people. You may be the biggest introvert in the world, but I guarantee there is a small spot in you that thirsts for connection to others, and when that thirst is satisfied, that's when the magic happens. "TEAM: Together Everyone Achieves More" – it's not just a overly used slogan, it's actually the truth. Many hands make for light work.

But with all this said, having the right team is make or break. That's why the discernment that Holy Spirit brings is so important. If Holy Spirit isn't scouting the proper people to your team, you may want to hold off on building a team. Also, if you are not aligned in certain core values, you may not be teammates – you may just be strangers passing by. The key to picking the right team is alignment and season. Not everyone you meet is meant to be on your team. All teammates are aligned in a main common cause, goal or outcome.

Understanding the importance of team is a important characteristic of being a kingdom kid, and so is maximizing your abilities. I will venture to say that it is virtually impossible to live to the max without a team. Teams have further reach. How can you truly reach all those you are called to with only your two arms? You need more arms, eyes, legs, brains. Collaboration is a superpower that we all need more of. The true blessing of working in a team is that it can fill in the gaps. When your team is constructed properly, you will have all your weaknesses covered by people in your team. For example, if you are not the best at working with finances, you would collaborate with a financial expert, and the same goes for any of your deficiencies.

Have you noticed that even the superhero movies have gone away from the "I can do it all by myself" model in recent years and really started adopting the team mindset? Good teams are built on good teammates, so make sure that in your pursuit of team, you are also building yourself to be a good teammate as well. I tell all my players that if you are not in the gym on your own, then you are not being a good teammate, because you don't care about your team enough to get better on your own so you can contribute something special to the team. We are stronger together – all my work and experience combined with yours makes us a powerhouse. Why have one superpower when I can have a team full? If you haven't noticed, this particular point in maximizing me really excites me as a coach. Another benefit of having a team culture and mindset is the ability to leverage your relationships at the highest levels, and that brings me to my next step.

## 3. LEVERAGING RELATIONSHIPS

This third step is extremely important. It's similar to point 2, but this takes the team aspect to a greater level. Yes you will leverage your relationship with Holy Spirit, and yes, you will leverage your relationship with your team, but what about the relationships with strangers – people who are non-permanent, seasonal or, even less than that, simply passersby? One of the greatest abilities to have is to be able to clearly determine how long each individual is supposed to be in your life and when the grace for that relationship has run its course. Oftentimes, we get in a lot of trouble by holding on to people longer than we were supposed to, not really valuing our seasons and the leveraging power of each meeting or encounter. By no stretch of the imagination am I saying to use people and leave them, but what I am saying is to consult with God for each encounter, for every conversation and every meeting.

Also, this does not require you to talk to or build with everyone you meet – some people are merely to meet in passing and keep it pushing. But there is a clear and underutilized opportunity in the space of networking. Most of us meet people every day, and most of us have squandered away opportunity after opportunity only because fear wont allow us to leverage our encounters. Most of the time, when we meet new people, if we would learn to ask the right questions and have the right conversations, we would receive valuable information from people we may never see again, but the seeds are lost because lack of conversation or proper interactions, i.e., pointless small talk. These are potential seed opportunities that are squandered away because of insecurity, fear or just plain old ignorance. You wanted to ask the question but thought it was too aggressive, while they may have been waiting for someone to engage them so they can pour out.

What about the relationships that become established but never meet their full potential because you are not willing to put your pride aside to ask for help or advice? The opportunity to leverage relationships is lost every day, and unfortunately, it's because of fear, pride, shame and insecurities, among other things.

The other unfortunate part is that people are willing to sacrifice their ability for potential substantial growth because they fail to leverage the people they come into contact with every day. One of the greatest things I've learned in life is that it costs nothing to ask. What's crazy is how many people would never ask, as if it would cost them their lives. Learning to leverage your relationships is literally like creating a revolving dream team. It's like live YouTube or Google. When you leverage your relationships, you're giving yourself a opportunity not only to receive the boost you need to maximize yourself, but also to plant seeds and give people the ability to leverage their relationship with you. Planting seeds is a huge part of living to the max that we will discuss later, but that opportunity comes from taking advantage of the opportunities around you in the form of relationships.

## 4. JUMP

One of the greatest hurdles we face in our journey of maximizing ourselves is stagnation – in other words, our inability to take leaps of faith knowing that we are, once again, heirs to the throne. This is very important to the DNA of a kingdom kid. The Bible says *"the just shall live by faith"* (Romans

1:17 NKJV); it also says *"it is impossible to please God without faith"* (Hebrews 11:6 NLT). If I know one thing, I know that God is not pleased when his children squander the gifts, talents or abilities we were created to maximize, and the only way to truly maximize those gifts is to live by faith.

But living by faith is not enough – the Bible says *"faith without works is dead"* (James 2:26 NKJV). Dead faith is purposeless. In order for it to have purpose, it must have works. I think of it like this: Works or actions are like faith on wheels. It takes movement, action, constant leaps and jumps to go along with what you believe. Now, I am not saying not to plan or have strategy. I'm actually saying the exact opposite – planning and strategizing is part of the work or the jump. For some people, the beginning of planning is the first jump. And let's be very clear, some people are meant to just come up with the strategies for other people to execute – again, that's why team is so important. But back to the jumpers, a.k.a. the workers, a.k.a. the kingdom movers. When will our actions become the fuel that makes the world run? We are not just Spirit-led thinkers, we are also Spirit-led doers.

## 5. TEACH

In order for a person to fully maximize himself, he must become a planter. All you are, all you will become, your full evolution and your ability to maximize yourself cannot be complete until the student becomes the teacher. It is now mandatory for you to mentor, give back, take a younger you and help them along. If you never give back or recycle, you are not fully committed to the full cause. Maximization is completed through duplication: Can you teach someone the process, the steps you are taking and will continue to take? Let's be clear, you have come far on your journey, and your journey will continue even further, but becoming a teacher is a crucial part. Maximizing you is not just about present, it's also about future. There is no maximization without full investment into legacy. There is no maximization if those around you don't pick up some of your contagious power. Being a true kingdom kid is having the ability to live a purposeful and influential life, and none of that can truly happen without giving back. Now, let's not look into this too deeply. I'm not saying you need to become a professor or a motivational speaker, but I am saying mentor, blog, write a book, start a podcast, be creative and plant seeds any way you can. It's not just the right thing to do, it's who you are!

# FEAR AND LIES

"If you follow the path with fear, you will
always trip over a few lies on your way."

I would love to paint the picture as if there were no
hurdles, as if the journey of a kingdom kid doesn't
involve valleys, but in all actuality, that's a very major
part of it. I would even venture to say that it's a pre-
requisite to being a true kingdom kid. I like to use
the phrase "There is no strength without struggle,"
and the struggle that most of us will face is the fear
and the lies. In order to become who God has called
you to be, you must first fight the fear that comes
with the unknown, and with that unknown comes
the lie of who people say you are versus who you

actually are. Not knowing who you are leaves room for Satan to lie to you about who you are. When we receive those lies, they produce doubt, and that doubt turns into fear when we are living with fear and lies. We are in a literal fight for our lives, living in constant battle with ourselves. The bondage that comes from the fear is crippling – we tussle with things that are not even really there.

A great example of this is that was when I was 12 years old or so, I was deathly afraid of basements. I don't know why and I don't know how; all I knew was I wasn't going in no basement without being accompanied by someone. The only problem with that was my dad had purchased me a new bike that year. It was literally my dream bike. I will never forget it – a gold BMX with all the racing stickers and pads, pegs on the front and the back. This bike was amazing. Just one problem: It had to go in the basement every night.

Now, I would go down there only when my dad was in the basement, and if I had to put the bike down there by myself, I would literally toss it down the stairs. I was very much willing to ruin the thing I loved so much all because of fear, until one day when I got my bike from the basement and my dad noticed that my pegs were damaged and my spokes were bent. He said, "You are not getting anything new until you learn to take care of what you have."

That day, I had to make a tough decision: face my fears or continue to damage my bike until it completely fell apart. So, after I was done riding my bike, I put it on my shoulder and proceeded to the dark, cold, smelly, scary basement. But I didn't just run back up the stairs – nope, I was facing my fear head on. I pulled up a seat on some boxes, and I sat down there in the dark for what felt like two hours but probably was only like five minutes. Everything I imagined happening to me in that basement didn't; every thought I conjured up in my head was fake. I had created my own fear to the point that I was willing to sacrifice something I loved. After spending those few minutes in the basement, my life changed forever. If I was afraid, I was not going to let fear control me, I was going to face it head on. And every time, it was not what I thought it would be.

I tell this story because in order for you to get to your full potential and truly become a kingdom kid, you will have to make a tough decision: Will you let fear stop you or ruin something you love, or will you face your fears head on and become a overcomer? Now, I'm sure there are things that come to mind when you're thinking about fear and the challenge of facing it. But I'm here to tell you that your fears are not yours to fight alone. God said to cast your cares upon him because he cares for you. God knows your fears, but remember who your daddy is and give them to him.

A few things we can take from this story and also see in our own lives: Most of the time, fear is made up of lies we tell ourselves or ideas that we make up or assume about a situation or experience. The key to defeating this or facing these fears is, first and foremost, real love. My love for my bike and getting future gifts allowed me to face my fears head on. True love always overpowers fear. Second is the ability to recognize that I made it worse than it was, without truly having a reason why. I didn't blame my fear on anyone, I owned my foolishness, and that allowed me to look at my life differently from that point. And lastly, I just went for it. In the previous chapter, I talked about jumping. That leap of faith that I needed to overcome my fear is the same leap I take in all that I do. It's actually the reason why I'm even able to write this book. It's the same leap I took to quit my decent-paying, secure job to become a entrepreneur for the last almost 20 years, for God has not given me a spirit of fear but of power, love and a sound mind (2 Timothy 1:7). Now take your leap.

No matter how scary it is, know that God got you.

# A CLOSER LOOK

*"A fool seeks information;
a wise man seeks understanding."*

Let's get specific on some of the characteristics of a kingdom kid. We spoke about this in previous chapters, but now I want to give you more clarity and direction on what these are. I strongly suggest that you mark the ones that align with who you are. Before we get in depth, I want to give you a slight disclaimer: You do not need to check off all these boxes to be a kingdom kid, but you should have a few.

It's very important that you understand the first characteristic and maybe the most important part of what a kingdom kid is:

## 1. KINGDOM KIDS ARE NOT FINISHED PRODUCTS

Kingdom kids are constantly growing and evolving. Kingdom kids love to be stretched and challenged as a part of their evolution. Their belief is that if you are not growing, you are dying.

## 2. KINGDOM KIDS ARE LIFELONG LEARNERS

Kingdom kids believe that learning is essential, not optional. We believe that learning is our lifeblood. We believe that knowledge is the beginning of wisdom, and wisdom is power.

## 3. KINGDOM KIDS ARE DOERS

Although learning is a vital part of who we are, it means nothing without activation. Kingdom kids love to learn, but they get even more excited about the application of the information.

## 4. KINGDOM KIDS ARE LEADERS

Some natural, some taught, but all are leaders in some way. I believe that in order to truly be a kingdom kid, you need to become a leader at some point, but I'm also the kind of person who believes that everyone leads, even if you don't know it. But there's a difference between leading and being a leader. True kingdom kids accept the role of a leader and enjoy the challenge of it. We usually lead from the front or by example, but we can also put on our coaching hat from time to time.

## 5. KINGDOM KIDS ARE INFLUENCERS

Kingdom kids understand the power and authority that is invested in them, so they don't take lightly their ability to influence individuals, groups or whoever. Being a leader also helps in this area. Being influential comes with great responsibility, because everyone knows "more is caught than taught." This characteristic of a kingdom kid is easily one of the most important.

## 6. KINGDOM KIDS ARE GIVERS

This is another one that I feel is a non-negotiable when talking about kingdom kids. Kingdom kids understand that one key principle of the kingdom is charity or giving. Kingdom kids understand that seed and harvest is a huge principle of the kingdom: You reap what you sow, meaning you get what you give. The more you give, the better your life will be.

## 7. KINGDOM KIDS ARE KIND

This is one that I'm sure we can all say may be the hardest, but it needs to be a high priority. To be a kingdom kid, you must always understand that you are representing the King. This means you are a direct reflection of him. There are a number of scriptures in the Bible that talk about God's kindness – see Titus 3:4 or Isaiah 54:8, just to name a few.

## 8. KINGDOM KIDS ARE VISIONARIES

Kingdom kids are always thinking about what the future can look like as well as the possibilities of now, and asking how we can make something better. We are the type of people that can see ourselves and others as greater or better than they currently are. Kingdom kids see the bigger picture, the whole scope – that's one of the main components that fuels them and gives them hope.

## 9. KINGDOM KIDS ARE COLLABORATORS

This is one of our calling cards, understanding that we are a body and the body has different parts. Each part is important, and they all work better together (1 Corinthians 12:12-27). Kingdom kids understand that no one is meant to do life alone. If you are a introvert or enjoy being alone, that's not the same – kingdom kids may enjoy being alone at times, but when it's time to get a task done, they think "collaborate" instead of "I can do this on my own." One of the reasons they think like this is because they are visionaries and they understand that only a small vision can be done alone – the big visions take a team.

## 10. KINGDOM KIDS ARE SEEKERS

We seek communion with God, we seek kingdom, we seek Holy Spirit. Kingdom kids are seekers of wisdom and guidance. Kingdom kids are always looking to improve; therefore, they are always seeking ways to do just that.

## 11. KINGDOM KIDS ARE INNOVATORS

We believe innovation should come from the vision-holders, the leaders, the creators. If we serve the greatest Creator, then we too must be great creators. It's in our blood – we were born to invent, to discover the never seen, to innovate the solutions through our direct connection to Holy Spirit.

I hope you were able to find yourself in that list, but more importantly, if you did find yourself, I hope you are inspired to do more:

- Seeking
- Collaborating
- Innovating
- Learning
- Leading
- Giving
- Loving
- Influencing
- Growing
- Envisioning

All while being kind.

My hope is that you will continue to activate these qualities here on earth, that the kingdom kids will take their rightful positions at the head of the places where these traits are most needed.

C H A P T E R 8

# KINGDOM KIDS VOCABULARY

*"Your heart will always
be revealed by your words."*

1.  **Kingdom mindset** – A way of thinking that is
    congruent with the kingdom of heaven, thinking
    the way God thinks, a open and influenced mind
    built by the word of God and influenced by Holy
    Spirit. The highest level of thinking, thinking from
    a level of authority, dominion and power. Doing
    unto others as I would want done to myself is
    kingdom thinking. Seeing a potential problem
    as a opportunity for growth is kingdom mindset.

2.  **DNA (Do Nothing Accidentally)** – Kingdom kids
    live intentional lives; we move with purpose,

on purpose. We understand that all things are connected and every action has a reaction. We understand seed and harvest, and we honor God's process by planting God seeds to harvest Good fruit. Our movements are guided, calculated and precise. We operate with pinpoint accuracy. We are technicians, physicians if you will, here only to fulfill our Father's will for our lives.

3. **Light and Salt** – This is what kingdom kids are called to be, bringing flavor and illumination to dark and bland places This is a absolute requirement for the title of "kingdom kid."

Sunday is for celebration; Monday through Saturday is for representation, being the ambassadors that we are called to be for the kingdom, living lives that reflect the essence of God, the heart of God. Our calling and our faith must be greater than what we do on Sunday, greater than the three songs and sermons that are preached behind the four walls of the temples that we worship at together. Our lives must be lived with greater purpose and responsibility on Monday through Saturday. We have been tricked to believe that a walk with God is most impactful around other believers, but we are called to bring flavor and light to the world every day, not just on Sunday.

Of course iron sharpens iron, but then what? Are we supposed to continue to sharpen each other every day, or are we supposed to use our sharpness to cut through the world's broken systems? I think it's so funny how we have these testimonies that usually, if not always, happen outside of church about what God has done for us on our jobs, and when the Lord saved us from the paths we were headed down, the path of destruction, and God has done all these wonderful things, and we can't wait to get to church to share our testimony with believers who have also experienced the goodness of Jesus. And yes, I think it's important to share the victories, but why do we bring our outside testimonies inside the church? Why don't we share our testimonies of how real God is in our lives with those who probably need to hear our testimony more?

The Great Commission is to share the Good News into all the earth, but instead we pass war stories and victories back and forth through the sanctuaries, so much so that I have a few people's testimonies memorized from the church I grew up in. I know who used to be what and how they got delivered; I can tell their story better than they can. And although it may bless me to hear it the first time, there are people who are missing the goodness of the Lord through your testimony because your salt and light are in the wrong place. It's like putting a lamp in a place that is already well lit instead of the dark place that needed your light.

The greatest thing the kids of the kingdom could ever do is be in the place God has called us to be. It's one thing to find your purpose; it's another to be in the place of purpose, the place where your purpose matters. What happens to most of us is we learn the calling that God has on our life, and then we chase after the place where he wants us to use that calling, missing the opportunity right in front of our nose: the life we are already living, the jobs we work, the schools we attend, the natural platforms that we already have to be the salt and to spread the Good News. We forsake those places we are called to and instead pursue a place in a building full of people seeking and living the same way.

I want to take this moment to encourage you, now that you have done the work, to discover your calling, your divine purpose. Now that you are a kingdom kid, be intentional about your location, about who you deliver your salt to and who your light is impacting, because how you use what you got is actually more important than having it in the first place. God is looking for men and women who are good stewards, not just over their finances but over their gifts, talents and purpose. When you misuse what God has given you because you're in the wrong place to use it, not only do you miss out on a opportunity to grow, but you hinder yourself by selling yourself short of the potential that comes with positioning.

I remember when I asked my parents to buy me a mountain bike, their first response was "Why, what's wrong with the bike you have?" It was an almost brand-new Mongoose – back then, that was the street bike to have. My answer was simple: "I like it, it's cool." It was really because I had seen a kid with one in a movie, and I fell in love with the big rugged tires, the springs, the shocks, the cool colors.

So my parents said, "If you really want one, your birthday is coming up – that's all you're going to get." I was like, "No problem." I got my mountain bike, and I loved it. I would ride that thing around my neighborhood and I thought I was the man, until one day, my boy challenged me to a race. We jumped on our bikes, and my brother said, "Ready, set, go!" We both took off, and he not only left me in the dust, it was *bad* – like, it felt like I wasn't moving at all, although I was pushing my hardest. We got to the end of the street and I said, "Dang, why is your bike so much faster than mine? You must got that thang souped up." He said, "No, I'm just on the right surface for my tires. Your bike is made for dirt and rocks – that's why it's called a mountain bike." He said, "You had no shot at beating me on the street with that bike." Blew my mind. I went home and told my parents what happened, and they said, "We thought it was weird when you asked for a mountain bike, knowing that where we live is city paved streets and your other bike is made for the street, but we figured you had to learn on your own."

What I learned from that experience is that just because you see someone else with something doesn't mean it's for you, and you'd better make sure you pay attention to where they have that thing that you want – your location determines what you should be riding with. Also, ungratefulness will always have you looking at someone else's bike instead of loving your own. Comparison is the killer of callings – why covet someone else's gift when you have used yours to the max? Being a person who uses what they have the way God intended is really important to your kingdom duties as a kingdom kid.

# C H A P T E R 9
# FAITH ON WHEELS

"Action is faith with wheels."

Now, what kind of coach would I be if I didn't leave you with some action steps, some very achievable goals that you as a kingdom kid can immediately implement in your life? One of the greatest characteristics of kingdom kids is our ability to take action – our "just do it" mentality. Before I give you these action steps – or, as I like to call them, action arrows – I first want to encourage you to believe you can achieve these things in your life. Too often, we are told all the things we shouldn't do and never given the alternatives, or we are only told what is out of our reach. Since both of those are my personal pet peeves, I want you to know you can achieve anything you set your mind to. As corny as that sounds, it is 100% the truth.

With that said, these action arrows may not all be for you, and by no stretch of the imagination am I telling you to do all of these. These arrows are either for you to shoot into action or to spark ideas for what could possibly be action arrows for you. This is your light bulb moment, if you already haven't had it, or it's the start to the rest of your life living as a kingdom kid.

# 15 ACTION ARROWS FOR KINGDOM KIDS

## 1. START EACH DAY THE RIGHT WAY

The way you start your day will directly influence the rest of your day. I know, I know, this sounds so cliché, but you will be so surprised how many of us start off our day by taking in some bad news, some gossip on Facebook or Instagram, instead of acknowledging the giver of life and the gift of another day. Even as I'm writing this, I'm thinking about how big of a deal this is and how much this shapes your mood and your interactions throughout the day. If you want to be a kingdom kid, it starts with how you start your day. Remember, kingdom kids are intentional about the details. I promise you, starting your day off this way will make a huge difference in your life. Not to mention, the start of every day is the start of everything. Start with influence, start with power, start with direction. Start your day with gratitude and watch how your life follows the way you start it.

## 2. BE MINDFUL AND INTENTIONAL

Do things that are thoughtful. You are not in the "living by the seat of your pants" crew – you don't just do what you feel. Be thoughtful, pay attention and carry yourself as one who has put great thought into how you move. One of the things I like to do to be mindful and intentional is to monitor how I address people What am I calling them? Am I using adjectives that are empowering and respectful? Another example of being mindful and intentional is listening to people with great reverence to what they are saying. This is a very good way to practice being aware, mindful and intentional. It is the way of a kingdom kid.

## 3. TAKE REFLECTION BREAKS

This action arrow is one of the most important. Oftentimes, we as people just go through life without ever stopping to reflect. I've found that the greatest people are those who understand themselves – they know their strengths and weaknesses, and they are very much in tune with the power they need to succeed. Reflection breaks are literally check-ins with yourself and with God. They can look like prayer, or even look like a water break. The key to reflection breaks is to take them as often as you can to avoid burnout, and also to avoid having to restart something because you have not been taking the proper time to reflect or just check where you are. I don't know about you, but I personally hate having to do something over again because I didn't stop to reflect and evaluate during the process instead of waiting to the end.

## 4. GIVE YOURSELF SPACE TO BE CREATIVE

A true sign of kingdom is creativity. Remember, we are a reflection of the King of the universe. God's whole existence is creating, and if we want to be really specific, it's creating where there was nothing. That is something that I am convinced all God's children have: the ability to create. Not only do we all have the ability, we all get the urge. When I say "creativity," most people think of painting, drawing or building, but there are millions of ways to be creative – what's yours? (And yes, you can have more than one.) Goal 1: find it. Goal 2: express it. Remember, as kingdom kids, we are called not only to be creative but to be innovative, meaning it's okay to spend time throughout the day dreaming, using your imagination, thinking of ideas and inventions. Think about how many things you have thought about before they ever came out, and how much money you could have made if you were more willing to be creative, imaginative and able to execute on ideas.

## 5. TRY NEW THINGS

For most of us, this is a tough one. We are, for the most part, creatures of habit. But like I tell my 11-year-old son, how will you ever find new things that you like if you don't ever try new things? Think about it: What does it really cost you to just try new things? Really nothing. The tough part is that we find something we like or we find a way that works, and we lock those things in because it prevents us from being disappointed or wasting time. But how many times have you had that one thing you always eat, and today it just isn't as good as it normally is? Or you normally drive a certain way to work, and today there's construction and now you have to go a different way? You're trying to figure out why that makes you so mad. I will tell you – because it's breaking up your routine. And that's why trying new things is so important; it gives you options and makes you more versatile and flexible. one of my favorite sayings is "A flexible man never gets bent out of shape." Now, before you go off on your trying-new-things journey, be sensible and know this does not apply to everything, so please don't go off and get a tattoo on your face and say "Coach Mel said 'try new things.'" Coach Mel is talking about new foods, new clothes, new places, new hobbies, new types of movies, new ways of saving, new ways of organizing and things like that.

## 6. BE OPEN TO LEARNING

With trying new things comes learning new things, and this is a major key to being a kingdom kid. Kingdom kids are always and forever learning, and therefore, we are always growing. Learning keeps us sharp and moving. When you are open to constantly learning, it keeps you from being stagnant and complacent. I have never met a person who was learning and bored at the same time. I also want to be very clear: The beginning to learning is first being open to it. That's why I'm saying "be open to it," because when you are open to it, you can find learning opportunities anywhere. I am a firm believer that when you stop learning is when you stop growing, and when you stop growing is when you are dead. Kingdom kids are lifelong learners who are always open to learn from anyone, anywhere, anytime.

## 7. INVEST IN YOURSELF

This is another practical, self-explanatory thing that we should all do. We don't all do it, but for one who is a reflection of the King and stands in dominion, authority and power, investment in yourself is mandatory. This investment that I want to make sure I'm clearly communicating is spiritual, physical, mental, emotional, from what you are reading to what you are putting in your body. How do you treat yourself? Are you resting or just sleeping? Are you exercising your mind, soul and body? Are you taking yourself out to dinner and a movie? Have you ever paid for coaching or training? Have you looked into therapy? What courses/classes have you signed up for? This is all self-investment. Paying money, time or energy to build yourself is so important, so don't skip this one. Do you have a coach? Do you have mentors (more than one)? Who's your pastor, your big homie, your accountability partners? These are all investments that need to be made.

## 8. INVEST IN OTHERS

This one is very touchy for some people, seeing that most of us have been burned by someone. I want to be very clear that the investment I'm talking about is the one that comes without conditions. I want you to invest in people out of the kindness of your heart, and if this is something that is difficult for any reason, start off small and work your way to a place where you naturally desire to see other people succeed. This is crucial to your own success – being sold out to others' goals and achievements is like a farmer being dedicated to the seeds he plants in the ground, knowing that at some point the harvest he leaves in the ground in the form of seeds will eventually feed him, his family and his family's family.

Remember, it doesn't matter what the person does with your investment; it only matters that you gave it. This could be as small as an encouraging word or as big as a financial seed – not that an encouraging word is small, but for most people, that is easier to part with. As you are planting these seeds, make sure that you are not looking for anything in return – and I mean anything, not even a thank you. This investment is a act of kindness, an act of obedience and selflessness. Your reward will come from heaven, but you are not even doing it for that. Another way we can invest in others is sharing, whether it be something you learned or something you have extra of or no need for. Be someone who invests by sharing. Giving of time and resources is a kingdom principle, and those you invest in are jewels in your crown. Focus on you legacy by focusing on your reputation – this is what's important to one's life.

I want to take a small break here. I'm sure you were looking for some "spiritual actions" or things that seem more spiritual, like prayer, fasting or reading your Bible. Although I do recommend these things, I purposely chose other things to show you how God things, kingdom things, spiritual things come in a lot of different forms. The things that I named are spiritual things, but most people don't count them as worthy because they are not done in the church. But the fact is, they shouldn't only be done in the church, and the action arrows I have named up until this point should be used and implemented in your life wherever you go.

## 9. WRITE

I'm not saying you need to write a book, although I strongly suggest it. I'm saying just write when things come to your head. Write in a journal, or even just on scrap paper. Even if it's just for a season, documentation is so important. It also helps with arrows 3 and 4, reflection and creativity. You never know where some writing can take you, and you may not realize how extremely therapeutic it can be. With the advancements of tech, if you are someone who does not enjoy putting pen to paper or typing on a key pad, there are some great talk to text options that serve as a great tool for getting what's in your head out and scratching the creative and communication itch that we all have. This exercise of writing has been the spiritual springboard to some of the greatest inventions, speeches and sermons. Think about it like this: Have you ever had a great idea and then it slipped your mind? What if that idea sparked the next big thing in someone else's mind, but you lost it because you didn't write it down? You could have changed your life and your family's life with one idea that went from paper to action. Writing is where it all starts.

## 10.  SHOOT YOUR SHOT

This is similar to the arrow of trying new things, but this one is specifically talking about overcoming fears and apprehensions around rejection – asking for things you wouldn't normally ask for, applying for things you wouldn't normally apply for. The thing I need you to understand is that kingdom kids shoot their shot. We ask the tough questions; we ask the girl everyone thinks is out of our league out on a date. I'm encouraging you to shoot your shot – just try, just go, just show up, just ask, just call, just pay it. I need you to find yourself saying a lot, "What's the worst that can happen?" Try, attempt, go. Shooting your shot is in all actuality the very essence of faith on wheels – shooting your shot *is* the wheels. It's putting God to the test to honor his promises by actually attempting instead of settling back. Do you know how many things we miss out on because we simply won't ask, won't attempt or won't shoot our shot? No more will we have not because we ask not; we will shoot our shot.

## 11. TAKE THE LEAD

The Bible calls us the head and not the tail. It is our responsibility to lead when we see opportunities to lead. We need to write our names on the list, raise our hands, be at the front of the line. For kingdom kids, not leading is not a option. We understand that our actions and who we are will lead one way or the other. Let's be clear, the greatest leaders have balance – they know when to lead and when to follow. But even that is being a good leader, teaching folks that even when you are a leader, you know how to humble yourself and follow when the situation calls for that. The world could always use more great leaders, more great men and women with integrity and humility. It doesn't matter if you are born a leader or built into one. What matters is that you are in your right position when it's time to lead. Even if you don't consider yourself a natural leader or a leader at all, there will be a time when your area of expertise may come up, and that will be your time to shine for the kingdom and lead. I'm a firm believer that you also must give yourself opportunities to practice leading. You may be a natural leader, but with anything and everything, we should practice, and growth should be our goal even as a leader. So lead!

## 12.   GIVE

To be more specific, give things of value. Become a person who enjoys giving, one who enjoys blessing people. This one may be tough for some people – we have been taught to get, get, get. I'm telling you, the kingdom requires of us the complete opposite: give, give, give. Make it a lifestyle, practice it. Start by giving away things you have no use for, then upgrade to things you really want and care for. Someone is reading this right now and saying, "Why would I ever give away something I want or need?" That's a fair question, and the answer is threefold: 1) because you want to be a blessing to someone; 2) because you are a kingdom kid and kingdom kids are givers; and 3) you give because you can! And that in itself is a blessing. I'm not saying to start giving things away that you need; I'm saying to start by giving out of your abundance and work your way up to giving as a lifestyle. When you start on this journey of giving, you will soon realize how fun and gratifying it is to be a blessing to others, not to mention the spiritual significance and impact this will have on your life. Kingdom kids are led by love, and love gives.

## 13. FINISH!

I almost left this one out because it sounds so simple and a little condescending, seeing as no one starts anything with the intention not to finish. But to us, this has to more important. Finishing everything we start is valuable to our reputation as kingdom ambassadors. When you finish things, you are also saying you are trustworthy, committed and reliable. A person who finishes what they start, whether good or bad, is strong and to be respected. Most of us can testify how much easier it is to start a thing than to see said thing all the way through to its completion

– and let's be honest, starting things isn't easy either. But I know how many things I've started that I wanted to run away from instead of finishing them. No matter how big or small the task is, be a finisher. There are people who will say it doesn't matter, just move on to the next thing. And they may be right when you are not representing someone greater than you, but when you represent the kingdom, your reputation of strong character and integrity is crucial and of the utmost importance. And if you are someone who completes things and people can contest that your word is your bond, this is important – so important that I couldn't leave this one out.

## 14.   BE GRATEFUL

Always take time to acknowledge how blessed you are, using words like "thank you" on a regular basis. This gratefulness limits selfishness and comparison. Gratefulness is a brick in the foundation of contentment. Also, being grateful keeps you at throne, the feet of God – gratefulness produces praise, praise produces presence, presence produces power, power produces increase, increase produces gratefulness, and the cycle continues. When we are grateful, we are shifted away from ungratefulness, which leads to striving, greed and discontentment.

When you are grateful, you are merely recognizing how blessed you are and creating space to receive more through honoring the giver and not the gift. Being grateful is simply deciding to focus on what you have and being thankful for it instead of focusing on what you don't have.

## 15. SUBMIT / YIELD

Pride comes before a fall, but grace is given to the humble. When you learn to be submissive and yield to the power of God, you are saying two things: "Lord, I'm in need of you, and I'm humble enough to know that and act like it." Submitting to God is impossible without submitting to the people that God has placed in your life. This is the hard part – we are called to submit to the authority that is placed in our lives. The reason why we are afraid to submit is because we are scared of being taken advantage of, not understanding that when we submit to authority, we are submitting to God, and we have to understand that God will protect us in our act of submission. Also, submission says to God that his will is what you need in your life more than your own. Unwillingness to submit to God's will is disobedience – there's no cute way to say it. Ask yourself this question: Is your will and your agenda more important than God's? Once you ask yourself this important question, then ask yourself: Are you willing to give up the power that comes from being in God's will through disobedience? That's why yielding and submission is crucial to being a kingdom kid.

# END NOTES

I hope what God has shown me to share with you blesses you. This is something I believe is crucial to edification of the body of Christ, but also to the fulfillment of God's plan to establish his kingdom here on earth though his children. We have been entrusted with a lofty task, but I believe we are up for it. We are the remnant – yes, you and me. If you have read this book to this point, you have a responsibility, and that is to be the salt, to be the light, to be the remnant to represent the kingdom of God at the highest level with the power that is invested in you. You have been drafted, enlisted, chosen. So, your first task is to share this book of instructions with other like-minded individuals, other kingdom kids, because remember, we are better together. Your second task is to continue on this journey to spread the power of the kingdom through your acts of charity and humility. And lastly, be a kingdom kid wherever you go, leading by example, helping to change the narrative about what it looks like on this side of grace and why we are called to be kingdom kids.

Made in United States
North Haven, CT
14 November 2022

26735708R00046